Series Editor Nigel Trevena

ISBN 0 906899 16 8   *First published 1985*
2nd impression 1988

Volume Three

GREAT WESTERN BRANCH & MAIN

by P. B. WHITEHOUSE

Design...
Printed...

© Millb...

No part...
form o...
permiss...
Publis...
ATLA...
PUBLI.....
Waterside House, Falmouth Road
Penryn, Cornwall TR10 8BE, England

Gone, but not forgotten...

INTRODUCTION

Those of us who were fortunate enough to know the Great Western Railway *per se* took it for granted. We went to school in chocolate and cream coaches pulled by rather austere looking 2-6-2 tanks which when clean, and sadly that was not very often, sported polished copper capped chimneys and gleaming brass safety valve covers; we waited eagerly to see which King was on the Paddington express, we groaned when the next pick up goods had a familiar pannier tank at its head and we kept out of the way of the pill-box hatted station master. But the Western was great. Its stations were generally clean, its staff sported carnations in their buttonholes, its ticket collectors were more strict and

the countryside through which it ran could be truly lovely — Cornwall, Devon, Somerset, the Cotswolds and the Vale of Evesham. Not to mention the Cambrian Coast and the very particular appeal of the South Wales valleys.

But the pattern has now changed. Many were lucky to see the Indian Summer of the late 1950s when locomotives and coaches came near to being painted in the old livery and the old branch lines were almost intact. The Western's route to the north west and Wales was still its own then, Snow Hill Station, Birmingham a reality and newly built Castles, Halls and Countys hard at work. Now this is a dream, though by dint of good fortune some of our most renowned railway photographers experimented with the old Kodachrome I film and got results which today are

treasures: pictures not just of main line expresses, but branches, sheds and artifacts. This generation owes them a considerable debt, for in that last decade the railway was still there almost in its original form, something that today's schoolboy could not imagine. Now, preserved and gleaming Great Western engines make a fine sight, but it cannot be the same. Thank you then to those who have stolen time from wives and work to let us record the following scenes for posterity and today's enjoyment.

One last word of appreciation. Without the help of John Edgington at the National Railway Museum and Nigel Trevena, neither the captions nor the pictures would have been as well chosen.

PBW

FRONT COVER: No.1004 *County of Somerset* climbs up through the Golden Valley to Sapperton tunnel, which is about 300 yards ahead. The black lined out livery of the engine together with the coach colours give a date in the early 1950s; certainly prior to April 1957 when the locomotive was fitted with a double chimney. Sadly, no County class engine survived the holocaust. *P. M. Alexander/Millbrook House Collection*

BACK COVER: A Calne branch train from Chippenham passes Hazeland behind 0-4-2 tank No.1458 (ex 4858). The whole train is ex GWR, with the locomotive newly painted in the mid-1950s lined out green, an embellishment never carried in the old company days. The red painted wooden bodied auto trailers are unaltered apart from livery. The Calne branch used push and pull trains in true Great Western fashion, working chimney first from the junction and often returning with the engine in the middle towing a Harris Sausage van trailer. *P. M. Alexander/Millbrook House Collection*

TITLE PAGE: Collett 0-6-0 pannier tank No.3794 takes the 12.30 pm Exeter to Tiverton train beyond Cowley Bridge on 2nd December 1961, almost two years before closure on 7th October 1963. *Peter W. Gray*

LEFT: The power of the Great Western: immaculate single chimney King No.6002 *King William IV* heads a running in turn near Corsham in the early 1950s. *P. M. Alexander/Millbrook House Collection*

In the far west

TOP: A holidaymaker's view of the Western in 1961. The St Ives branch is open today, so this view of Carbis Bay would still be possible albeit without the lovely plume of steam. The heavily graded and twisting branches from the Great Western's main line to Penzance down to the Cornish fishing villages needed powerful short wheel-based locomotives and were thus ideal for Churchward's 45XX class 2-6-2 tanks. On summer Saturdays, loads were sometimes heavy enough for the locomotives to work in pairs, but on 19th August 1961, No.4570 (one of the 1924 built batch) is on its own with the return empty stock. *Peter W. Gray*

Clay from Goonbarrow

RIGHT: China clay was, and indeed still is, one of the mainstays of Cornish freight traffic, sadly one instance where countryside preservationists are at odds with the railway. Light but strong, the Western (but not Great Western) 16XX class pannier tanks filled a useful niche for some of the branch workings as can be seen by No.1664 arriving at St Blazey with a train off the Goonbarrow branch on 13th July 1961. Although this class was not actually constructed until 1949, it was an updated version of the old and tried 2021 class with the same wheel diameter. It was the last ever independent Great Western design. *Peter W. Gray*

Bodmin branch pastoral

ABOVE: Backed by Polgeel Wood, another 1924 built 2-6-2 tank, No.4569, heads the 3.24 pm Wadebridge to Bodmin Road train near Grogley Halt on 10th September 1960. Both this branch and the ex London & South Western line out of Wadebridge closed to passenger traffic on 30th January 1967, the latter location being the haunt, in its very last years, of 16XX 0-6-0 pannier tanks and famous until 1962 as the last home of the LSWR Beattie 2-4-0 well tanks. A Mecca for enthusiasts, Wadebridge station could provide a feast in the form of GWR, LSWR and SR locomotives. *Peter W. Gray*

RIGHT: Square tanked 1915 batch 2-6-2 tank No.4552 shunts at Bodmin General station on 27th May 1961, once again with a train of Western gold, Cornish china clay. Amid the early flowering rhododendrons of the far south west, this is still very much a Great Western scene, no flat bottom track, no foreign brake van and a real Churchward engine. Take note, too, of the covered water tower, the rail built buffer stop with its warning red bullseyed oil lamp, the traditional stone goods shed with the loading gauge outside, plus the goods wagon in the siding. Today the pick up goods is dead and almost beyond memory. *Peter W. Gray*

Waiting in the sun

LEFT: Moorswater shed on the Looe branch at noon on 2nd September 1961 with one of the later 2-6-2 tanks, No.5573, sitting outside adjacent to the water column. The engine carries the Newton Abbot number 83A whereas one would have perhaps expected 83E St. Blazey of which Moorswater was a sub shed. The relief fireman reads his paper inside the shed door.
Peter W. Gray

Royal working in Devon

BELOW: Perhaps the best known as well as the most versatile of the Great Western's branch lines in the south west was (and in preserved form, still is), that from Aller Junction, just beyond Newton Abbot, to Kingswear, with a link to Brixham going off at Churston. One of the happy memories of many enthusiasts was the sight of Castles and Kings climbing up from Goodrington to Churston with heavy holiday trains including the Torbay Express. Normal passenger traffic was in the hands of either 45XX or 51XX tanks. On 30th March 1962, No.5153 heads the Kingswear portion of the 2.30 pm ex Paddington:

the make up of the train is of particular interest as there are three types of stock; the local branch set to the fore, then the normal through corridor coaches and, at the rear having conveyed HRH Princess Margaret to Torquay, a saloon, possibly No.9001 now preserved. *Peter W. Gray*

Still trains to Brixham

ABOVE: Almost impossible to believe today, Churston station on 11th March 1960. Apart from the cast numberplates on the smokebox doors, the red paint on the auto coach and the ornate *Cornishman* headboard, the scene has changed little from GWR days. On the left is the Brixham push and pull train and in the passing loop platform No.5055 *Earl of Eldon* (originally *Lydford Castle*) with the up express bound for Birmingham and Wolverhampton via Bristol, Gloucester, Cheltenham and Stratford on Avon. March weather did not encourage cleanliness. *Peter W. Gray*

Torbay bound local

RIGHT: Another Torquay line train, this time the 12.05 pm Exeter to Paignton, enters Kingskerswell on 4th May 1957. The three coach train is all corridor stock still in early BR 'blood and custard' livery whilst 2-6-2 tank No.4178 (built in BR days in November 1949) is black with no lining. *Peter W. Gray*

Traditional to the end

LEFT, TOP: Purchased for preservation two years later, Churchward designed but Collett built 2-6-2 tank No.4555 approaches single platformed Coryton station on 23rd June 1962. The train is the 12.40 pm Launceston to Plymouth and the whole scene gives a glimpse of a typical ex GWR south west of England branch. Great Western features are seen in the wooden ground frame hut to the left of the picture, the corrugated iron lamp hut on the platform, plus the station seat, lamp and nameboard. True to tradition, the branch or local train headlamp, carried on other railways at the top of the smoke box or coal bunker, sits neatly on the centre bracket above the buffer beam. The Launceston branch closed on the last day of 1962. *Peter W. Gray*

Enthusiasts' farewell

LEFT, BOTTOM: Bedecked with bunting by the local Women's Institute, Lustleigh station on the Moretonhampstead branch welcomes the South Devon Railway Society's *Heart of Devon Rambler* on 6th June 1960. This was very much a reflection of the enthusiast scene of the period when trips over freight lines or last trains were almost a norm. Although 2-6-2 tank No.4174 (again, one of the BR built locomotives) has its number on the buffer beam this is scarcely Great Western style as it also carries the word No. and the headlamp in its incorrect position on the bunker top. Note the good GW economy of old rails serving as posts for the station nameboard. *Peter W. Gray*

Station in the landscape

RIGHT: A pastoral scene at Thorverton in South Devon on 8th June 1963. On the left, 0-6-0 pannier tank No.3659 leaves with the 5.48 pm from Exeter St Davids whilst 0-4-2 tank No.1466 waits in the station with the 5.15 pm from Dulverton running trailers first; the leading vehicle carries the name *Thrush* painted on the panel below the centre windows. The branch connected the ex GWR main line north of Exeter running via Tiverton to the line from Taunton to Barnstaple which it joined at Morebath Junction Halt. Again this is a picture of the past. The Exe Valley branch is gone, closed on 7th October 1963, so this was the last summer. But the whole scene is now an anachronism for, today, who sees a line of empty wagons standing by a hand crane; at their head a neat stone built weigh house? Or for that matter, the wooden gated private siding with loaded wagons waiting for the day's pick up goods? The whole station is, of course, fully signalled with a small wooden box stuck on the end of the stone station building, whilst the adjacent station master's house is one of the perks of the job.

Peter W. Gray

Push-pull practice

But other tracks extended east of Tiverton. These linked that market town to the west of England main line at Tiverton Junction, with one intermediate station, Halburton Halt. This short branch outlived the Exe Valley line by just one year, closing on 5th October 1964. Collett 0-4-2 tank No.1471 takes the 2.22 pm Tiverton Junction train into the halt platform on 24th March 1962. Close study of the photograph shows normal GWR auto train practice with the driver sitting at the front of the bow fronted coach, his hand on the brake, whilst the fireman looks out of the loco cab watching for the platform. The driver's regulator control was connected to the loco by a series of rods and this, plus the brake handle, was all he had. It was the fireman's job to notch up, blow the whistle, work the injector and do the actual firing. *Peter W. Gray*

Waiting at Culmstock

ABOVE: The other branch out of Tiverton Junction was that to Hemyock, very much in Devon dairy country with milk traffic forming an essential part of its income. As with the Exe Valley branch, standard 0-4-2 tanks were the motive power. On 3rd November 1962, with Devon still leafy, the gates at Culmstock are being closed to road traffic whilst No.1421 is about to leave with the 12.09 pm to the junction. The station nameboard is pure Great Western. Services to Hemyock ceased on 9th November 1963. *Peter W. Gray*

Rain at Yeovil

LEFT: Yeovil Pen Mill on a dull 30th May 1964. The main line to Weymouth sweeps away to the left whilst the branch to Yeovil Town and on to Taunton is to the right. The two trains are headed by BR standard 4-6-0 No.73042 and GWR 2-6-2 tank No.4591, both under the control of newly installed upper quadrant signals. A piece of the new cut off route to the west of England, that between Curry Rivel Junction and Athelney Junction, was originally part of the Yeovil Town to Taunton section. Yeovil Town closed to passengers on 2nd October 1966 but the branch to Cogload and Taunton went two years earlier on 15th June 1964. *Peter W. Gray*

Now just a memory

RIGHT: With its windows boarded up, the Cotswold stone station building at Malmesbury stands forlorn but complete in May 1966, almost fifteen years after closure on 10th September 1951. Contrary to belief, some uneconomic country lines shut long before the swing of the Beeching axe and, sadly, Malmesbury was an obvious contender. It was once said that the Great Western was a railway for gentlemen linking the tradesmen of London and Bristol through country estates. Perhaps it was, but the railway blended well into its surroundings with its buildings almost indistinguishable from those of the sometimes remote hamlets and villages which it purported to serve. The Society for the Preservation of Rural England would have had little cause for complaint. *K. Cooper/ P. B. Whitehouse Collection*

Prairie turn

BELOW: Small wheeled 2-6-2 tank No.5554 scuttles a Westbury to Swindon two coach set between Thingley Junction and Chippenham during the early summer of 1961. Fully lined out and painted in the green livery of the late 1950s this is one of the last hundred engines built between 1927 and 1929 with larger sloping tanks adding a further 300 gallons to their capacity. *P. M. Alexander/Millbrook House Collection*

Cross country

Another BR built 2-6-2 tank, No.4161, heads the 4.00 pm Gloucester to Hereford train on 15th May 1964. This cross country route served as a market town link for well over a hundred years, opening on 1st June 1855 and closing on 2nd December 1964; it was steam worked to the end, in its last years by Churchward 2-6-0s as well as the 51XX class tanks. It met the Gloucester, Chepstow, Newport line at Grange Court Junction. Ross on Wye was the junction for the pretty Wye Valley branch to Monmouth, worked for years by the ubiquitous 14XX class 0-4-2

tanks usually with a single auto trailer. Monmouth, too, was a minor railway centre and a terminus for two further cross country lines, one to Chepstow and one to Pontypool Road on the Newport, Abergavenny and Hereford line. The two branches along the Wye Valley closed on 5th January 1959 with a 64XX class pannier tank working to Chepstow. The GWR railcar operated Pontypool Road (via Usk) section was shut as early as 30th May 1955. Private car ownership — growing as it did in the 1950s — sealed the closure of all these cross country routes.
M. Mensing

Long since closed

ABOVE: Titley Junction station on 6th May 1961. This was the junction for the short section to Presteigne running north from the Leominster to New Radnor branch. Closed to passenger traffic on 7th February 1955, freights behind a wheezing Leominster 14XX 0-4-2 tank still worked up till 6th July 1959. Titley was an excellent example of a small railway junction, important in itself but situated almost nowhere. *K. Cooper/P. B. Whitehouse Collection*

Black Country local

RIGHT: A service locally called 'The Bumble Hole': auto fitted pannier tank No.6434 propels a Dudley to Old Hill train near Darby End Halt with the 6.41 pm ex Dudley on 14th May 1964. The single compartment coach adapted as an auto vehicle is unusual as the old trailers enabled the guard to issue tickets en route to passengers joining at unstaffed halts. This connecting link was one of the three ways in which Dudley citizens could reach Birmingham, changing trains at Old Hill to pick up a local from Stourbridge Junction. The other routes were via Swan Village and Handsworth Junction to Snow Hill or the ex London & North Western line to New Street via Dudley Port. *M. Mensing*

Classic rural junction

A supreme example of an important Great Western Railway junction sited almost nowhere and called by the name of a road to indicate the nearest town or village. Pontypool Road served as a jumping off point for the South Wales valleys, Newport, Hereford or, cross country east, to Monmouth and Ross on Wye. It was also a considerable centre for freight and many GWR *Toad* brake vans had the magic words 'Pontypool Road' painted on their side planks. Still there today, but with its importance considerably depleted, what is left of the station hardly acts as a museum to its past.

As late as 20th August 1962, all seems complete and the spotters are having a field day. No north to west express is making a mandatory stop so no large engine is visible though there are ex Great Western coaches in abundance. In the platform is 0-6-2 tank No.6605 with the 1.10 pm to Neath whilst 2-6-2 tank No.5164 takes water at the column. *Peter W. Gray*

Along Welsh byways

LEFT: Taken from the window of the 4.10 pm Neath Riverside to Brecon headed by 0-6-0 pannier tank No.3768, this photograph shows Cradoc station on 20th August 1962. By its appearance, Cradoc was then an unstaffed halt and sadly neglected at that, with paintwork peeling and a grass grown platform. However, Great Western cast iron letters are still solidly screwed onto the station nameboard. Once part of the Neath and Brecon Railway, Cradoc passed into Great Western ownership at the 1923 grouping of railways, when one considerable point of interest was its method of working. In Neath and Brecon days, arrangements had been made from the 1880s for the Midland Railway (who controlled the nearby Swansea Valley Railway) to work all services and this was continued by its successor the LMS until the end of 1930. In the good or bad old Victorian days, access to the black diamonds of the Welsh Valleys was eagerly sought and the Midland, via Hereford and Brecon, held on tight. It is reasonable to assume that after 1930 the LMS thought twice for, like its near neighbour the Abergavenny Merthyr line of the erstwhile LNWR, the Neath and Brecon's passenger services outlived their freight, closing as from 15th October 1962. *Peter W. Gray*

Three line terminus

RIGHT: Brecon station on the same day with No.3768 on the 6.20 pm return working. Brecon was the terminus for three lines, the Neath and Brecon, the Hereford Hay and Brecon (ex Midland) and the Mid Wales to Moat Lane (ex Cambrian), the latter two bifurcating at Three Cocks Junction. Whilst the Neath line saw standard 57XX pannier tanks the other two showed considerably more variety with Dean Goods and ex Cambrian 0-6-0s on the Moat Lane line until the BR standard 2-6-0s took over in the early 1950s. Dean Goods, Midland 0-6-0s or ex L&Y 0-6-0s worked the Hereford line. Note the porter with the pigeon basket on the trolley. *Peter W. Gray*

The Barmouth shuttle

Taken from the road bridge on the edge of the town, this photograph shows Dolgellau (once Dolgelly) station looking towards Ruabon on a stormy 25th August 1962. The scene is very little altered from Great Western days except that 0-6-0 pannier tank No.7405 has replaced the normal auto train headed by a 14XX 0-4-2 tank, even a chocolate and cream painted clerestory camping coach sits in the platform bay. The train is the 1.41pm local to Barmouth and the engine, sporting its headlamp in the correct position (this was then the LM region) at the top of the bunker, has just run round its coaches, part of the day's shuttle operation to and from Barmouth. The branch shed was at Penmaenpool a mile or so down the line. Although it is high summer, note the concrete coal bunker next to the fire devil at the end of the left hand platform — a very Great Western appurtenance to ensure that the water column does not freeze up in winter.

Dolgellau was originally an end on junction of the Great Western from Ruabon on the main Shrewsbury to Chester line and the Cambrian from Barmouth Junction — later Morfa Mawddach. *Peter W. Gray*

A King in flight

A west of England express nears Twyford just after leaving Sonning Cutting with a mixture of red and chocolate & cream stock around 1960. No.6027 *King Richard I* was one of the earlier Kings to be fitted with high superheat and a double chimney (August 1956) resulting partially from the sad performance put up in the locomotive trials of 1948, when No.6018 *King Henry VI* made the poorest showing of all on its own road, causing some critics of Swindon practice to regard the Kings as an outdated design. The fitting of the four row superheaters and double chimney improved coal consumption considerably. *P. M. Alexander/ Millbrook House Collection*

A King at rest

The coaling stage at Wolverhampton Stafford Road shed with No.6017 *King Edward IV* — a Stafford Road engine from February 1959 until withdrawal in July 1962 — having her tender topped up. The Western used this somewhat archaic system of coaling to the end. Wagons were shunted up to the stage and unloaded into small tubs which were rolled out onto a plate overhanging the loco tender. With the arrival of the 4,000 gallon tenders, their additional height necessitated the installation of a small electric hoist in most larger stages to allow a clear drop. *K. Cooper/P. B. Whitehouse Collection*

Majestic line up

LEFT: Three Kings — Nos.6000, 6023, 6024, have escaped the breaker's torch so perhaps one day the preservationists will duplicate the scene shown here; three Great Western flagships ready for the road at Wolverhampton Stafford Road in the late 1950's. This was the last shed for sixteen of this thirty-strong class. *P. M. Alexander/Millbrook House Collection*

Westbound express

BELOW: King No.6021 *King Richard II* heads the 4.15 pm Paddington to Plymouth via Bristol in the late 1950s. The train is approaching Thingley Junction out of Chippenham and No.6021 was then shedded at Plymouth, Laira (83D) shed. *P. M. Alexander/ Millbrook House Collection*

Memories are made of this

A Bristol to Paddington express approaches Chippenham near Thingley Junction headed by No.4097 *Kenilworth Castle*, one of the earlier members of this famous class built in June 1926. Taken at a particular favourite spot of Philip Alexander's, this Kodachrome I transparency is one of his finest, showing a Western Region train in full flight through the Wiltshire landscape, the engine clean and resplendent with sparkling brasswork and burning its Welsh coal with virtually no smoke. The engine, though very much as originally built, has a Hawksworth straight sided tender. The train is in early BR 'blood and custard' livery with as far as can be seen, mostly ex GWR stock: giving a date of the early to mid 1950s. *P. M. Alexander/Millbrook House Collection*

When she still served

ABOVE: One of the first two Castles to be fitted with a double chimney, No.5043 *Earl of Mount Edgcumbe* is near Chipping Sodbury with a South Wales to Paddington train, soon after passing through Sodbury tunnel. Like the Kings, many of the Castles were fitted with four row superheaters and double chimneys thus improving their overall efficiency but somewhat marring their appearance. Withdrawn in September 1963, No.5043 went to Woodham Bros. yard at Barry for breaking up but was purchased ten years later by the Birmingham Railway Museum as spare parts for No.7029 *Clun Castle*. When originally fitted with a double chimney in May 1958 No.5043 was one of the engines used on the Western Region's really crack express, The Bristolian. *P. M. Alexander/Millbrook House Collection*

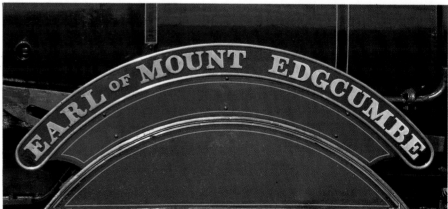

RIGHT: Nameplate of No.5043. Built in March 1936, the locomotive was christened *Barbury Castle* but was renamed in September 1937. The Earl nameplates were initially carried by the first reconstituted 'Dukedog' 4-4-0s (Bulldog boilers on Duke frames) but it is said that the nobility were not amused at their titles residing on what appeared to be ancient pieces of machinery so those fitted with such plates had them removed and the class became nameless. 'Dukedog' No.3200 (Nos.3422 Bulldog and 3288 Duke), built in May 1936, carried the plate *Earl of Mount Edgcumbe*, a good Cornish name from the old *Duke of Cornwall* class. *K. Cooper/ P. B. Whitehouse Collection*

Shadows of Brunel

Sidney Gardens, Bath, in the summer of 1960 with then single chimneyed No.7020 *Gloucester Castle* heading a Bristol to Paddington express. This was just into the Raymond Regime on the Western when chocolate and cream sets were ordered to be broken up and mixed with the then standard red (almost LMS) livery. Even so, BR built No.7020 is in pristine condition and the train, very Great Western with the board Paddington Bristol and West of England above the corridor windows of the leading vehicle. Whilst not a total Brunel scene, when looking at the stone walls and the flat arch of the bridge one goes far back into the history of the Great Western: twelve years into Nationalisation, the track is still bullhead, the motive power almost 1920s and junior neatly dressed in a jumper and shorts, Meccano Boy fashion, sits on the parapet and waves hopefully to the loco crew. *P. M. Alexander/P. B. Whitehouse Collection*

West to north

LEFT: One of the 'aeroplanes', No.5071 *Spitfire* (*Clifford Castle* until September 1940) about to leave Bristol Temple Meads for Crewe and Manchester in the mid 1950s. No. 5071 received a double chimney in June 1959. This was one of twelve engines patriotically renamed for aircraft during the Battle of Britain and 1941 periods of World War II. Note the words 'Castle Class' under the actual name on the splasher plate: similar plates were carried on converted Stars. Bristol Bath Road shed, situated at the south end of Temple Meads station, housed a number of Castles and Bristol was often used as a loco change over point.

Although termed expresses, west to north trains were in many ways overgrown semi-fasts as they stopped at most of the market towns once north of the Severn Tunnel, though admittedly these were some miles apart. Note the early BR lettering on the ex Great Western Coach W1655W. *P. M. Alexander Millbrook House Collection*

Section clear ahead

RIGHT, TOP: The daily running in freight turn from Stoke Gifford sidings to Swindon leaving the relief road at Chipping Sodbury station; it was obliged to wait here for an up South Wales express to pass through. The locomotive is Castle class No.7005 *Sir Edward Elgar*, one of the batch built just after World War II in June 1946 and named *Lamphey Castle* until August 1957. Note the covered water tower, the lovely bracket signal and the flat bottom track on the down road. *P. M. Alexander/P. B. Whitehouse Collection*

Smoke, ash and steam

RIGHT: Two Castles at Carmarthen in March 1962. On the left, with a single chimney, No.5054 *Earl of Ducie* — chosen as one of the elite to haul the last leg of the final Plymouth to London steam trains in May 1964 when it was hoped to achieve 100 mph near Little Somerford. This failed and No.5054 was duly broken up while the other two participants Nos.4079 *Pendennis Castle* and 7029 *Clun Castle* were saved. On the right, with a double chimney, is No.5027 *Farleigh Castle* with wheel tyres apparently down to their last turning and due for withdrawal in November. Note the ashman and the generally dirty condition of the shed. *P. M. Alexander/Millbrook House Collection*

Halls of fame

LEFT: No.4993 *Dalton Hall* of 81D shed (Reading) waits at Bristol Temple Meads station with a west of England excursion. The train has just arrived and the spotters in shorts and long stockings are checking the locomotive in their books: a very typical Saturday scene on any main line station of the 1950s. By the look of the smoke, it appears that the fireman has placed some coal in the box during the last minute or so: the engine is blowing off (contrary to good practice in stations) and the coal will dull matters down a little. Just as well if there is an inspector about. *P. M. Alexander/Millbrook House Collection*

ABOVE: Modified Hall class No.6962 *Soughton Hall*, built in April 1944 but not named until October 1946 because of war time economy restrictions, leaves Hullavington station on the Swindon to South Wales line with the daily running in freight turn from Stoke Gifford. Note the Collett type tender and the excellent external condition. Here, too, the down track is flat bottom: a sign of things to come. *P. M. Alexander/ Millbrook House Collection*

RIGHT: The nameplate of No.4976 *Westwood Hall*, built in February 1930. The livery is early BR mixed traffic locomotive black, lined out — in theory — with a straw colour, but Swindon lining was much nearer the old Great Western's orange: a pseudo London and North Western Railway livery scarcely appealing to the Western Region authorities. The Halls reverted to green (lined out) with the change of policy to non-centralisation in the mid 1950s. *K. Cooper/ P. B. Whitehouse Collection*

On the Cornish main

A summer Saturday relief express to the 4.50 pm Penzance to Crewe via Bristol and the Severn Tunnel crosses Liskeard viaduct on 6th August 1961 behind an unknown Grange class 4-6-0. Note the Looe branch running to the right of the picture. Surprising as it seems today, August Saturday traffic was still very much at its height at the end of the 1950s and beginning of the 1960s, some branch terminii — such as Newquay in Cornwall or Kingsbridge in Devon as well as Paignton and Torquay — having through Paddington trains. During weekdays one changed at the main line junction. There were times when the branch services climbing steeply from the seaside resorts to the main line on the spine of the hills were double headed, usually by 45XX tanks or sometimes 57XX panniers. The stock, empty for 6 days, was stored somewhat wastefully but it *was* a service.
Peter W. Gray

Black Grange

The 10.55 am Ilfracombe to Wolverhampton (via Gloucester and Cheltenham) train at Stratford on Avon on 11th August 1956. The engine taking water in readiness for the climb up to Bearley is No.6868 *Penrhos Grange* painted in BR mixed traffic black which does not enhance its appearance. Boiler pressure is well up as it needs to be if a pilot is not being taken. Stratford shed, out of sight to the left of the picture, housed not only 2-6-2 tanks for the local services but also some 22XX 0-6-0s as passenger pilots when necessary. These would be coupled in between the train engine and the stock to ensure that the train engine driver was in charge and controlled the brake. *K. Cooper/P. B. Whitehouse Collection*

Freight from Wales

Churchward Mogul No.6312 near Rodbourne with an up South Wales freight. Maids of all work, the basic 43XX class was a great success as true mixed traffic engines, as much at home at the head of a Birmingham Snow Hill to Barmouth Saturday excursion as they were on a local from Hereford to Gloucester or on a main line freight. Altogether the class consisted of 342 engines though with the coming of the Granges and Manors these had been reduced by Nationalisation to 240. Many were sent overseas with the British Forces in World War I. Numbers varied from 43XX through to 93XX; the separately numbered series relating largely to weight distribution or differing boilers. *P. M. Alexander/Millbrook House Collection*

Bound for the coast

The Cambrian Coast Express ran Mondays to
Saturdays from Paddington to Birmingham,
Wolverhampton and Shrewsbury (in its latter days
behind a King all the way) reversing there for the
journey through Welshpool and Moat Lane Junction to
Machynlleth where it split. The main portion went
south to Aberystwyth whilst the remainder set sail for
the coast-line, Aberdovey, Towyn, Barmouth, Harlech,
Portmadoc and Pwllheli. From Shrewsbury the motive

power was inevitably a Manor and sometimes at peak
times two Manors, both (prior to handing the Cambrian
over to the LMR) kept spotless. The coast-line train
could have almost anything at its head, a 63XX class
2-6-0, a Dukedog or maybe two Dukedogs or perhaps
a 22XX class 0-6-0 or combinations of all — except
the Mogul which was powerful enough to do the job
alone.

Coming home on the up train, it was a more
difficult task as the climb to Talerddig lay ahead.

When the load was too heavy for one engine,
Machynlleth shed provided a pilot as far as the
summit. However, this is the down train but still
double headed by 2-6-0 No.6362 and No.7823
Hook Norton Manor carrying the Cambrian Coast
Express headboard. The date is uncertain but by the
condition of the engines, it looks like being in LMR
days. *P. M. Alexander/P. B. Whitehouse
Collection*

All stations local

2251 class 0-6-0 No.3217 enters Wilmcote station with the 8.43 am Stratford on Avon to Leamington Spa (General). It is 15th May 1964 and steam will soon come to an end with Stratford shed closing. Note the headlamp in the correct position at the base of the chimney on No.3217 and the leading coach originating with the LNER. In the refuge siding at the rear, both the train engine No.7926 *Willey Hall*, then only just over thirteen years old, and the banker blow off impatiently. *M. Mensing*

Heavy freight

One of the later but still basically Churchward 2-8-0s, No.3850, with a heavy freight slogging up the 1 in 300 gradient from Wooton Bassett to Badminton, passing Rodbourne between Somerford and Hullavington. Note the banker on the rear. The 38XX series were up to date versions of the Churchward 1903 design, being built between 1938 and 1942 with outside steam pipes, side window cabs, short safety valve bonnets and smoke box door lamp irons. They did, however, retain their lever reversing gear, unusual for such modern construction. They were very typical Great Western engines, simple, hard working and well liked. *P. M. Alexander/ Millbrook House Collection*

Outside framed veterans

LEFT: Two Dukedogs, Nos.9004 and 9014, at Llwyngwril — south of Fairbourne on the Cambrian Coast line on the first Saturday in October 1959. They have worked up to Towyn from Shrewsbury with an AGM special for the Talyllyn Railway Preservation Society and then north to turn on the triangle at Barmouth Junction before returning light to Machynlleth for servicing. The rolling stock was left at Barmouth for cleaning. *P. B. Whitehouse*

On Cambrian shores

BELOW: Clouds hover over Cader Idris as a very dirty 90XX Dukedog class 4-4-0 leaves Barmouth bridge with a through train from Shrewsbury in May 1953. It is the Whitsuntide holiday Saturday and the five coaches are still full in spite of stops at Aberdovey, Towyn and Fairbourne. If one swapped the red and cream of the coaches for chocolate and cream, this is very much a train as seen at the end of the 1930s, including the white spare headlamp kept on the bracket at the side of the smokebox saddle.
P. B. Whitehouse

The legend re-appears

The record breaking No.3440 *City of Truro* in steam at Wolverhampton Stafford Road shed on 16th June 1957, the year of its return to service. The occasion was a Stephenson Locomotive Society Midland Area special to Swindon works. Rescued from the small ex LNER museum at York and overhauled at Swindon, due largely to the then Western Region Chairman Reggie Hanks, *City of Truro* was put into regular service on Didcot, Newbury and Southampton trains to earn her keep, as well as heading numerous enthusiast specials journeying as far north as Glasgow.

On withdrawal from service for the second time the engine was placed in Swindon Museum along with *Lode Star*, Dean Goods No.2516 and one of the later pannier tanks. With the coming of the 150th anniversary of the incorporation of the Great Western, *City of Truro* was removed from the museum during July 1984 for overhaul in readiness for the following year's celebrations, the work being carried out by the Severn Valley Railway at Bridgnorth. *K. Cooper/P. B. Whitehouse Collection*

Really the end

Scenes at Three Cocks (junction for the Hereford Hay and Brecon and the Mid Wales lines closed 31st December 1962), Chipping Norton (closed 31st December 1962) and Princetown (closed 5th March 1956), each in its own way representing the end of an era caused by the greater convenience of road transport. In their day, Great Western branches were well ordered, carrying everything that the country people needed and becoming an integral part of the countryside they served. The Western ran its branches with dignity and care; they were safe if slow but, above all, they were run by staff who cared.

K. Cooper/P.B. Whitehouse Collection (2)
Peter W. Gray